Recycle and Save

Recycling   2

We recycle   4

Recycle bin   6

Garden bin   10

Glass bottles   14

Glossary   16

Recycling

When we turn  into

a  it is **recycling**.

When we turn  into

a  it is recycling.

When we turn  into

a   it is recycling.

Recycling helps to save our planet.

We recycle

We can help to recycle at our house.

Recycle bin

Here is our recycle bin.

It has a yellow lid.

We can put these bottles in our recycle bin.

We can put this paper in the recycle bin.

We can put this box in
the recycle bin.

Garden bin

Here is our **garden** bin.

It has a green lid.

We can put
garden rubbish
in the garden bin.

These flowers can
go in the garden bin.

These **branches** can go in the garden bin.

Glass bottles

I can take my glass bottles here.

They will take
the bottles and give me
some money.

Glossary

 branches

 garden

 recycling